Check out the

"Free Man Beyond the Wall"

podcast hosted by

Mance Rayder on

iTunes, Stitcher, Google Play, iVoox

and YouTube.

www.freemanbeyondthewall.com

Freedom Through Memedom

FREEDOM THROUGH MEMEDOM

THE 31-DAY GUIDE TO

WAKING UP TO LIBERTY

MANCE RAYDER

The most dangerous man, to any government, is the man who is able to think things out for himself, without regard to the prevailing superstitions and taboos. Almost invariably he comes to the conclusion that the government he lives under is dishonest, insane and intolerable, and so, if he is romantic, he tries to change it. And if he is not romantic personally, he is apt to spread discontent among those who are.

H.L. Mencken

Freedom Through Memedom: The 31-Day Guide to Waking Up to Liberty

Mance Rayder

Publisher Information

Copyright Information

Cataloging Information

ISBN-13: 978-1978400818

ISBN-10: 1978400810

Table of Contents

Ha! There is no table of contents. This "guide" consists of 31-days of commentary, and although I want you to read them in the order I wrote, I know some of you won't so I'm not gonna make it easy for you.

I will tell you that some of the days have more than one meme in them and the one on the top is the one referenced in my commentary. Any accompanying meme is of the same subject and may add clarification.

There's also a bonus section of memes after day 31 that will all be related to a subject I wrote about.

ENJOY!!

Foreword

Mance Rayder has mastered the art of the meme for the libertarian community. Rayder has a talent for challenging people's acceptance of previously held received truths and opening their minds to the contradictions they had overlooked. With a simple picture and an ironic note about the nature of political power and the ends it produces, Rayder takes on our culture's backwards assumptions about war and peace, taxation, guns, natural rights, democracy, patriotism, leftists and right-wingers and all their crazy deviations from principle and truth.

And most importantly, he's funny. And humor is the strongest tool for cracking through the thick skulls of the ideologically predisposed. May Mance Rayder's internet memes continue to discredit power for all time.

Scott Horton, November 2017

Preface

I'm fairly certain the first memes I experienced were on the once famous website Ebaum's World. I probably didn't know what to make of them at the time, but they were usually funny, and I would check back to the site often.

Enter Facebook. By 2010 my Facebook wall was a collage of memes considering most of my friends were either gun owners or libertarians. Those two groups were early to the meme party since both are constantly defending their individual rights.

Having no confidence in the electoral process, especially given the choices in the last general, in mid-2016 I felt the need to get the message of liberty out there. I climbed on my Twitter account (I rarely used it) and started posting "anti-statist" memes that I either made myself (a minority of them) or procured from other sources. Many of you reading this came along for the ride and I am grateful.

My podcast "Free Man Beyond the Wall" came soon after and as of the day I am typing this I have released 53 episodes. Two or three podcasts a week are entitled "My Meme of the Day" and can range from three minutes to six depending on how long I feel like ranting. I just select a meme and comment on it. That brings me to the "book" you are reading.

Years ago, I did accounting for a Christian book store and noticed that one of their top-selling genre of books were called "Daily Devotionals." They are laid out over a specific period (usually a month) and each day would normally have a bible verse plus a short commentary for you to contemplate. My assumption was that these were to be used in the morning.

This "Daily Devotional" uses the same premise but replaces a bible verse with a meme and the inspirational commentary with cold water to your face. In my mind this guide is perfect for any novice liberty seeker, that (L)ibertarian that needs to take the next step in abandoning faith in the State, or any voluntaryist/anarcho-capitalist/agorist that loves memes and frank commentary.

Some may ask, "When would you read this?" If it were me, it would be on the back of the toilet ready for that morning visit to the porcelain throne. Most civilized people may wish to keep it on their coffee table to read with their morning java/tea/beverage of choice. I would read the days "lesson" in the morning and start my day with a good "wake up call."

You will notice that some themes are repeated. I believe these are the subjects most vital to understanding the power the State has over us.

Using a 31-day period, I believe I have laid out a concrete argument for the abolition of the State, using memes and only a few paragraphs.

Freedom Through Memedom

<u>Day 1 – Uncomfortable Truths</u>

We should always start off the month with the most basic of facts. None of us have been "awake" long enough that we shouldn't hear it again and again.

Taxation is not voluntary and any action in which you are forced to participate, especially if the act takes what is rightfully yours by labor or natural right, is an act of violence against you and is WRONG!

If your neighbor Bob the Cab Driver came over to your house every Friday and demanded 30% of your wages for the week, you would probably get violent with him. How is it then that if Bob switches jobs and now works for the IRS that makes it OK? It doesn't! It never has, and it never will. (Later we will go over why even if Bob is an I.R.S. agent his actions are unjustified)

Reminder - If you choose to voluntarily pay taxes because you WANT to, that's fine. That does not give you the right to demand it of someone else.

Have a good day and never forget, "taxation is always theft."

Day 2 – If You Can't Do It, Nobody Can!

Anarchist: Do I have a right to take your things?

Statist: No

Anarchist: if I come back with a majority, can we then take your things?

Statist: No

Anarchist: so where does government get the right to take someone's things?

statist: because the majority agrees on it

Here's some truth you should think about every day. Much like yesterday's message about Bob not being able to demand 30% of your labor, this can be applied to any group or individual representing said group. This goes for any anyone seeking to take from you by force.

Think of the police. They somehow have the authority to stop a free man on the street and rifle through his possessions all the while raising their voices to him, or even subjecting him to bodily harm.

Do you have the right to do that? Does anyone? No? Then how has that right been passed to someone else? Magic? Or is it just wrong and a violation of natural law?

Have some fun today – Seek out someone you are comfortable with and attempt to explain the above truths to them. Be calm and respectful. Have your answers to their objections ready.

Liberty starts in the mind.

Day 3 – Free Speech is Non-Negotiable

Anyone trying to shut down free speech knows that their ideology is a lie so they must prevent you from exposing that. I have no problem listening to someone else's opinion, ESPECIALLY if I know it's dead wrong. Knowing that my ideology is moral and non-coercive helps immensely.

Free speech has been under attack since the beginning of time by people in power, those who seek it, or by those who just want to control you and your thoughts. Free speech has nothing to do with words on a piece of paper, you are born with the ability to say what you want. The only time an argument could be made that your speech is "damaging" is if you are directing an individual or a group of individuals to do harm against another's person or property. Even then an argument could be made that if the people choosing to follow the orders are doing so voluntarily you still could be without blame.

When you're having a conversation with someone about free speech and they say, "hate speech" has no right to be spoken and is not "free speech" what are you going to say? How much do your opinion and beliefs mean to you? If someone says punch all Nazis AND anyone that promotes free speech what will you do?

I know what I would do but that decision is up to you.

Do something out of your comfort zone today. Strike up a conversation with someone you would avoid. Know you have the truth on your side.

Day 4 – The Enemy is Always Ready to Pounce

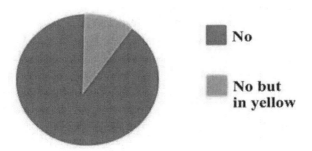

Ah the college student! The empty vessel wanting to be filled with knowledge. I mean that's what education is, correct? "Fill me with wisdom that I may show the world what I know!"

To make the statement that MANY college professors are either Marxists, or have Marxist leanings, would be news to no one that's paying attention. The odds are that the child sent off to university today will be assigned a great deal of Marxist writings including Marx himself.

What is the result? Many of people you encounter that are of college or Grad School age, or ones that were educated as such, have a place in their heart for communism/socialism. This leads to discussions about how great communism is and how it is the only fair system for the people.

That brings us to our meme. As someone that knows communism fails every time and causes mega-death and suffering, you will undoubtedly point this out. WAIT FOR THE BUT!

"But it just hasn't been done right" cries our hero of the people. But you know, don't you? You know the ego it takes to want to rework a system of death and destruction.

Remind yourself today that your wanting better for yourself, is what's best for everybody around you.

Day 5 – Guns are Your Private Property

This society has spawned a bunch of indoor cats, people that have no idea how to defend themselves if put in a life and death situation. The police have no mandate to protect you (read Warren vs. District of Columbia for a good education on the nature of law enforcement) and even if they did, their response time to active crimes gets them there to help below 5% of the time. Why would you rely on them?

Get yourself a gun and get yourself some training. I repeat, get yourself a gun and get yourself some training. You don't need 10 guns. I'm more worried about the man/woman that has one and knows how to use it.

Now to our meme. I would never tell anyone to break the law, that's on you, but if you live in a state where private gun purchases are allowed only buy privately. In the above episode of Walking Dead Negan knew exactly how many guns Alexandria had because someone kept a log.

Buy a gun privately, train with a professional and take you and your family's safety into your own hands. And NEVER register a gun! If you do make sure you have one or two more they don't know about. Guns are your private property and if they're yours, why should someone be allowed to take them away?

So ends the lesson for today!

<u>Day 6 – A Barrel of Rotten Apples</u>

Government actors are a part of the population.

Government actors are a part of the population.

Government actors are a part of the population.

Government actors are a part of the population.

Government actors are a part of the population.

Government actors are a part of the population.

Government actors are a part of the population.

The theory is that because people can't be trusted with freedom, so we need to have a government to control them. Ahem, where do we get these people from? From the same pool that "people need to be protected from." If the apples are rotten which do you pick to eat?

Has it ever occurred to you that evil people may desire government power so they can operate with impunity?

Day 7 - No People Have Ever Voted Their Way to Liberty

It's amazing how many humans believe that they are so much more evolved than animals. We look upon traps that are laid for seemingly intelligent creatures and shake our heads at how they can fall for them. When will they learn?!

These are the same people that fall into the same trap year after year, election cycle after election cycle. Trump ran on a policy of limited foreign intervention, basically only if he had to. Do you remember watching those rockets being launched against Syria not three months into his presidency? A great question someone snarkily asked afterwards was, "Did you really think you could vote away the Military Industrial Complex?"

The great Tom Woods has a quote that, especially in the Age of Trump, is empirically provable, "No matter who you vote for you get John McCain!"

No one that has been elected to office has EVER rolled back government. There is no change. Voting is the literal definition of insanity, "Doing the same thing over and over expecting a different result."

Do what you will, but expecting change because you pull a lever or touch a screen, is no better than belief in the tooth fairy.

Day 8 – Know Who the Real Thieves Are

THE HURRICANE HASN'T EVEN HIT AND ALREADY LOOTERS HAVE BEEN SPOTTED

Disasters bring out the looters.

Mayor asks for 8.9 percent property tax hike in the aftermath of Harvey

I would hope by now you are starting to realize who the real enemy is.

At the time I am writing this Hurricane Harvey has just devastated Houston, Texas and its surrounding areas, and Hurricane Irma is pointed directly at Miami, Florida.

I used to live in South Florida and am familiar with hurricane prep and all considerations that must be made while planning. One major one is looting. Looters come out of nowhere looking to steal anything that isn't tied down.

Now imagine if they had a license to steal your property. There are people that have free reign to steal your stuff and there's a picture of two of them above.

The brainwashed two-party slave will argue that one wants to do good with it while the other doesn't and vice versa but that doesn't negate the fact that first they must force you to give up your labor at the threat of violence.

When you watch the "news" and see that thieves have broken into a house or business and stolen property someone has worked hard for don't forget about the real professionals that have an army of volunteers with guns stealing your labor before it even gets to you.

Day 9 – Do You Really Want Rulers?

NBC4 Columbus ✓
@nbc4i

Study finds 16.4 million Americans think chocolate milk comes from brown cows #NBC4 nbc4i.co/2tva3At

By now you must know that at this point in history to have rulers over us is just plain psychotic.

Read the above headline and consider what I've said in the previous sentence. The uninitiated's first impulse would be to scream, "Damn it, people are idiots, we need someone to protect us from them. Give me government!!" There is no doubt that a good portion of the people are dumb. There's no denying it. But..........

Where are you getting these people to protect you? Is there some race of perfect super-humans I am unaware of that government and police have been neglecting to hire from?

If you want rulers, they are going to come out of the same pool of people that believe chocolate milk comes from brown cows and that putting a camera in a woman's stomach can help doctors see the baby during childbirth (a State legislator suggested this).

People are evil and stupid, why would you want them ruling over you?

Day 10 – The "Rights" Double Standard

When government does it:	When anybody else does it:
Enhanced interrogation	Torture
No-knock raids	Breaking and entering
Taxation	Armed robbery
Arrest	Kidnapping
Indefinite detention	Holding hostages
Education	Indoctrination
Making a campaign promise	Lying
Campaign contribution	Bribery
Defense operation	Aggression
Military occupation	Land theft
Security patdown	Sexual assault
National security	Spying on neighbors
Peacekeeping mission	Invasion
War	Mass murder

There are some subjects that must be discussed multiple times until people fully grasp them. The subject of the "double standard" when it comes to State actors and their actions is one that I think about every day. I remind myself to ponder it.

On the right of the meme is a list of actions that you and I will be thrown in a cage for were we to perform them. Yet when the "State actor" does it, it is normalized.

Let's look at what the State calls "Enhanced Interrogation." If they feel the need to get information out of a suspect they have been given the right (mind you, by people that do not possess that right to start with) to beat, maim and kill to get it.

What if your child were lost and you had a friend that said they saw he/she headed into the woods with a neighbor. If you took it upon yourself to do to your neighbor what the State does to their suspects, that same State would lock you in a cage. I know I am beating the horse to death but where do they get this right from if an individual or group cannot convey it? And why do you accept it?

Maybe it's because they attach a fancy phrase to it like "enhanced interrogation" instead of what it is....torture!

Day 11 – The "Consistency" Straw Man

This is one of my favorites and shows how narrow the minds of most people really are.

I believe in unfettered free markets which means I don't want a government or any authority, with a monopoly on force and law, to be able to make rules or regulations that they get to dictate and change at will. The market will always come up with its own rules that will undoubtedly pave the way for progress and innovation.

BUUUUUUUUT, that doesn't mean that I won't be able to look at the way a company is doing business and criticize them or flat out call them a fraud. That is free speech which also has its own checks and balances in a free market economy.

When someone engages in the type of argument in our meme they are purposefully being dishonest, or they are just plain stupid. A little prodding and it should be evident which.

Imagine this argument in practice. I sell tires, and someone does not like the fact that I offer free tire rotations for the life of the tire, so they voice their dissatisfaction in public. What happens? Do I call the police to have him arrested, or will enough people look at him and tell him to mind his own business, or if he doesn't like it don't shop there?

The above argument is among the more ludicrous you will encounter. Don't waste your time!

<u>Day 12 – "I Was Just Following Orders!"</u>

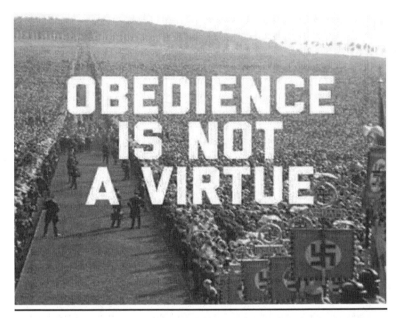

"I was just following orders" is the mantra of anyone that finds themselves on the wrong side of history.

How is it possible that murderous tyrants have been able to get so many people to obey them and march in lockstep? I believe that most people, from the day they're born, are raised in environments that teach them to obey "authority" and never question it.

Many factors lead to this. Nationalism is the most obvious. My favorite quote on nationalism is by Albert Einstein and he spoke it BEFORE the rise of Hitler. Einstein said, "nationalism is an infantile disease, it is the measles of mankind." That makes sense especially when you consider that people that are nationalists are generally taught it from a young age.

The much rarer trait is to see someone raised as a radical individualist. That's what I am trying to accomplish with this "devotional." My assumption is that most of us were taught to be nationalists no matter the country we were raised in. If we look at history, it is rare to see a nationalist that accomplished a leap forward in thinking. On the contrary, it is usually the man/woman that has chosen to think for themselves that pulls society beyond the dark days of the past.

Day 13 – The Tragedy of Comfort

(For the sake of this meme I am going to run with the narrative that the War for Independence was fought over a 2% tea tax.)

The only purpose of me using this meme at this point is to throw a bucket of cold water in your face. The next time you come back to this meme I want you to be angry.

Ask yourself why people back in 1776 felt it was so important to rebel over a 2% tax. Now ask why there is no rebellion when taxes combined for income, sales, auto, gasoline etc. are 40% and higher.

Do you have an answer? My first answer will sound foreign to most, but it has to do with comfort. Most people are just comfortable enough that their chains are only a minor nuisance. They chafe but hey, "I'm in the Land of the Free and the Home of the Brave!"

I will end with what I see as the major reason why we will never see a revolt while the status quo is kept; people fear loss. I'm not even talking about violent uprising here. What would happen if 10 million people refused to pay taxes. Answer the question, what could they do?

The greatest men acted even when they were in fear for their freedom, life, etc.

Day 14 – Mandatory Worship

Think about the things we've seen in sports the past few years. The NFL's ratings are down, and it is being attributed to lack of patriotism on behalf of some of the players. ESPN is suffering the same fate because they have consciously decided to have a far-left cultural message, as well as dismissing on-air talent that were openly right-leaning. ESPN openly supports the NFL players that are taking a knee during the National Anthem.

I think you know by now that I am an advocate of free association and if people choose not to watch something on TV I say good for them. Most TV is a distraction anyway, "Bread and Circuses" in my opinion.

Think about the reasons why though. You've seen the reactions, many are visceral. There's a huge hive mindset at work here. People have been conditioned to the point that it has been suggested that LAWS be passed that require standing during the National Anthem for not only the players, but for anyone in attendance! LAWS! Not rules handed down through the league, but code enforced by officers with guns. If that sounds insane to you, you're on the right path.

Ponder what they're asking for. Could you imagine not standing for the national anthem at a State-sponsored event in N Korea? Do you still think this is the "Land of the Free and the Home of the Brave?"

Day 15 – We're Halfway There, is The Problem Clear?

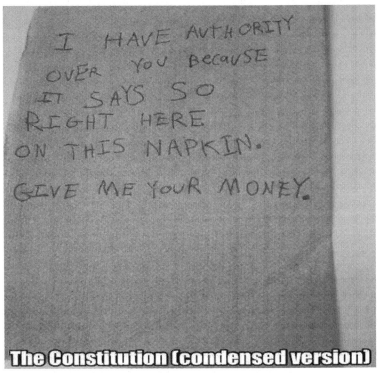

"Everyone has a right to affordable health care!"

"Everyone has a right to go to college!"

"Everyone has a right to own a home, it's the American Dream!"

We've all heard these. Some of us have even believed them, but do you honestly think the government can give this to you? Do you believe it's their job? I'm sure we are all familiar with the term "reform." It's a political term like no other in that it tells you that every government plan is a failure. Just about everything they do is "reforming" their previous mistakes that have caused massive debt and further dependence on THEM.

If you ran your life like they run government where would you be? Do you have a printing press to bail yourself out as they do? You would be destitute in the gutter. Yet people are brainwashed into believing that only government should run the "important" things.

To borrow an argument from the brilliant comedian Dave Smith, if government should be responsible for the most important things why don't we put them in charge of food? Is there anything more important for survival? How about shelter? What about clothes?

When you realize how much they screw up everything they touch, do you want them touching anything that we need to survive?

<u>Day 16 -Are You Afraid to Take a Stand?</u>

This is a popular picture that has been meme'd a thousand ways in recent history, but most people don't know the actual story behind the man portrayed.

According to his daughter, his name was August Landmesser and he was a worker at a shipyard in Hamburg, Germany. On the thirteenth of June 1936, the Nazi party was celebrating the maiden launch of a naval training ship and the workers were to be gathered to salute the occasion.

What most people who see this picture do not know is that by this date, August had a falling out with the Nazi party over the fact that he was having a relationship with a Jewish woman named Irma Eckler. His love for Irma was illegal and soon after he was sent to prison and later drafted into penal military service where he was killed in action. Irma was sent to a concentration camp where it is assumed that she was killed as there is no record of her afterwards.

August's story is a powerful one which raises the question; in the face of similar circumstances what would you do? Does liberty mean so much to you that you would be willing to make great sacrifices for it, or would you rather be comfortable, safe and one of the masses?

When people who allegedly love freedom mock you because you point out the failings of the government system and tell you, "if you don't like it LEAVE!", what would you do?

Choose well!

Day 17 – What Will You Do About Unjust Laws?

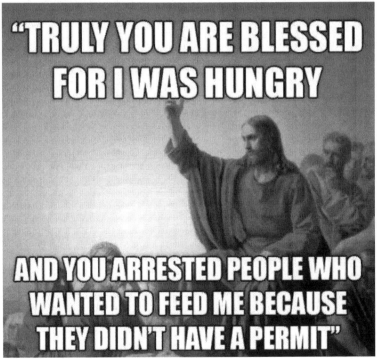

On January 08, 2017 the group, "Food Not Bombs" went out and fed the homeless in Tampa, Florida. Seven volunteers brought food that had been paid for privately and went about their business. Little did they know that they were breaking the law. According to local "Law Enforcement" (a very important term) the group was technically "trespassing" on "public land." They had neither acquired the official "paperz" or "permit" to perform their good deed.

I doubt that these Good Samaritans were either "voluntaryists" or "anarchists" but they refused to stop when asked saying that they were doing "the right thing." The "law enforcement" officers proceeded to arrest them but that didn't make them back down from their stance.

We have two patterns of thought here: what is "legal" and what is "right." How many people do you know that believe in their convictions so strongly that they will choose incarceration by the State over "freedom?"

The time may come for you to make a choice yourself, do you know what you will do? Have you ever thought about it? Do you think the time may be now?

<u>Day 18 – The Straw Men Continue…..</u>

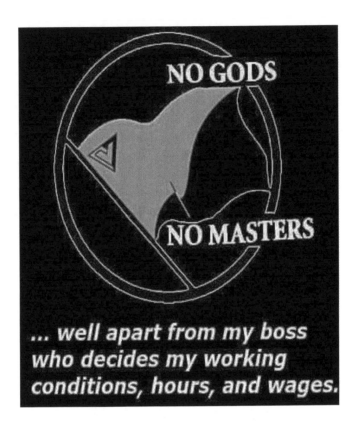

If you're looking at this in the early morning, please accept my apologies! No one should have to deal with a "Straw Man" this big, especially in the early A.M. hours. Yet here we are.

Recalling all that I have taught so far, I would hope that half of the people reading this would be able to immediately spot the flaw in this meme. The logo above is popular with voluntaryists and anarcho-capitalists. It speaks to the fact that no man has the right to tell another what he/she can do. We answer to nobody other than our conscience.

The critic that has added the words at the bottom is making a huge leap. With very few exceptions, people must work to survive. Even if someone were to go into nature to "live like our ancestors" (which arguably would be a much tougher life), they will WORK!

For the critic's words to be true you would have to be a slave. I don't know about you, but I've quit jobs I didn't like and immediately found a better opportunity whether it be pay, hours, location or just a more enjoyable environment.

Be ready for the inevitable "straw man," because if you desire liberty, it's coming!

Day 19 – They Will Attempt to Shut You Down!

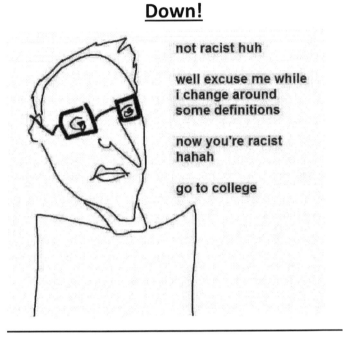

If I made the statement right now that this society is in a culture war I don't think anyone reading this would argue with me. I know that a lot of you would say that free speech is under attack, but understand that basic freedoms are as well. If Free Speech drops, everything goes away, and I mean everything!

When I went to college what seems like a century ago nobody was declaring, "you can't say that." On the contrary, free speech was encouraged and everybody was asked to speak up and say what was on their mind. That seemed to take a drastic turn in the last 20 years.

The meme above is an accurate depiction of what is happening on college campuses today. Any student that says something that is outside of the protective bubble they have put up is immediately shouted down and typically tagged a "Nazi." The theory is that if they can label you the worst of all things, the "racist Nazi," you are completely discredited and anything further coming out of your mouth is hate speech.

Even if you were to somehow "win the day," they will just change the rules and BOOM, you're a Nazi again!

This is not only happening on college campuses but many of these tyrants have graduated and taken up home in H.R. departments all throughout commerce. What will you do?

Day 20 – Zombie Replies

On the day Hugh Hefner died I posted a picture on Twitter with a quote in which he puts forth the idea that we own our minds and bodies, and for church or state to attempt to limit that, is inappropriate. A random Tweeter that didn't "follow" me deduced from the comment that if "his own mind dictated to him that he build a foundry on HIS property and it poisoned the area that would be perfectly fine." Mind you he'd be poisoning himself as well but...

This is the type of reply you come to expect when you wake up to the fact that you were born to be free of rulers and pursue what makes you happy. When you get vocal about it, these types of responses become the new normal.

The meme above addresses one of the most essential natural rights that you possess: the right to be left alone, or privacy. I remind you that it has nothing to do with a magical piece of paper and only YOU can defend it. A typical response when it comes to privacy, which the government says you must give up for the sake of "safety," is clear in the meme. Knowing what you know now, how would you respond if somebody responded as in the meme?

Day 21 – "The Law"

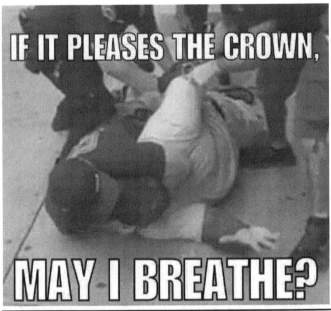

There is a saying amongst liberty minded people that you may wish to learn:

"There is no law so small that the police won't kill you for."

The meme above pictures the "arrest" of Eric Garner. He was standing in front of a Staten Island convenience store when NYPD officers walked up and accused him of selling "loose" (individual) cigarettes from packs that DID NOT HAVE A TAX STAMP.

Garner said he wasn't selling "loosies" and told the police he was tired of being harassed. One officer responded by attempting to put Garner's hand behind his back and cuff him to which Garner responded by pulling away. The officer then put Garner into a choke hold. Due to the choke hold and other tactics used by police Garner died. You can read the conclusions online. No officer suffered discipline. The autopsy is clear that the police broke "their own rules."

You read that right, Eric Garner was put to death for suspicion of breaking the tax code. People like to say that the worst that can happen to you when you don't pay taxes is jail time. It appears that some jurisdictions take their theft a little more seriously.

How do you see the death of Eric Garner?

Are you O.K. with law enforcement having the power of judge, jury and executioner?

Day 22 – Dealing With Economic Illiteracy

Let's throw a "straw man" back at them but not really.

If you spend any amount of time on social media, you have probably seen #Fightfor15. This references a "movement" that believes if the minimum wage is raised to $15 an hour somehow all "income inequality" will cease? Honestly the things I've heard from them are incoherent so it's hard to figure out what their end-game is.

The meme above is a direct response to #Fightfor15. It's a way of saying, "if $15 will do no harm to business, why not $50?" Why not $1,000?

Proponents of #Fightfor15 like to point to an outlier city that has raised the minimum wage and not experienced the eventual repercussions (yet!). They argue that raising the minimum wage everywhere is going to work because of this. If you've read any of the recent articles coming out of Seattle people are having their hours cut because the city decided to raise the minimum wage to $15 causing employers to turn full-time people into part-time people, or they cut the workforce and kept their best employees, trimming the fat.

When I ran a service-related business with several employees, on a very slow day I would send staff home early to save on labor. These were hourly workers that knew this could happen when they were hired. The price of labor will always dictate the price of the service or product. If you force an employer to pay his employees $6 an hour more, he will either cut his workforce or increase the price of his good or service, or both. This effectively cancels out the buying power of everyone's wage increase. This is logic, yet so many people struggle with it

Do you understand this well enough that you would be comfortable explaining it to a family member?

Day 23 – Private Property Revisited

Me: How would you abolish private property without initiating force?

Anarcho-communists:

woosh, there is no property

AnComs: "You can't protect private property without the state!"

Rooftop Koreans: "Dude how ahistorical can you be?"

For those who may not know what an "anarcho-communist" is here's a definition:

> *a theory of anarchism which advocates the abolition of the state, capitalism, wage labor and private property (though some strains retain respect for personal property) and in favor of common ownership of the means of production, direct democracy and a horizontal network of workers' councils with production and consumption based on the guiding principle: "From each according to his ability, to each according to his need".*

I mean, what could possibly go wrong? Does that definition make you want to ask a thousand questions? Leaving everything else behind, let's address property as it is the subject of the meme.

An example of "personal property" to the ANCOM is the famous "toothbrush," so you get the idea. What is "private property" to them? Owning a house or business, basically anything that generates profit. They hate the idea of somebody building something and keeping it to themselves, or charging somebody for its use. That's why in their "utopia" they must STEAL IT from you. You've heard the term "seize the means of production." Well that's what they will do with any private property.

And how will they do this? A question I always ask them is, "if you get your way what will you do with someone like me that desires private property, a business and profit?" Rarely will they answer directly but sometimes I'll get an honest one who says, "well, you will either comply or be dealt with." Must I explain what they mean by that?

Day 24 – How You Will Not Win Your Freedom

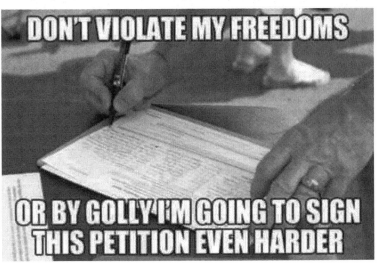

The picture in the above meme was taken on October 1, 2017, the day that the Catalan region of Spain went to the polls to "vote for their independence" from the motherland. Spain had warned Catalan that if they went through with the vote Spanish police would be sent there to shut it down. Spanish police were not able to prevent the vote but not for a lack of trying.

This whole episode is a perfect example of "statism." On one side you have the STATE telling a group that desires autonomy that this "breaking of our law" will be met with violence. But why do I have an arrow pointing to a voter/protester? Did the Catalonia Referendum declare individuals free or would it set up another State? Do you see where I'm going with this?

How can we ignore the fact that no people in history have won their freedom through voting? Not to mention, if you know that you have been threatened with violence, why would you not be ready to meet it in kind? How do you plan to protect your newly voted for "freedom?"

Catalan as a State has declared themselves independent from Spain but remember, Catalan is a mass of individuals that desires to trade one massive State rule for a smaller, but destined to expand local rule. They have traded a giant monster for a smaller one. How will an individualist truly feel free?

<u>Day 25 – Time For a Laugh Break</u>

If you're already active in the "Liberty Community" you probably laughed as hard at this as I did. It's probably the best "inside joke" we have. Libertarian/Voluntaryists love to discuss every possible subject down to its minutia and then argue about the 1% we don't agree on.

I think it's a shame that it upsets a lot of people in that discussion/debate/cursing (maybe not cursing so much) is like sharpening the edge on your mental sword. I don't use the imagery of a sword flippantly. From the subjects we've previously discussed, it is clear the struggle against statism ends up being literal "life or death" for some. The more that you know the better you can handle yourself.

Remember that when discussing liberty and people get serious or tense. Try to dial it back a notch and tell a joke to alleviate the stress. We're all in this together and that person that you're debating with may be a great ally in a day when you need people on your side!

Day 26 – The Ignorance of the "Leftists"

Semi auto
AK trigger

Automatic
AK trigger

Which of the two pieces on the
left do I file down to create
all the extra pieces on the right?

Whenever there's a crime in which multiple people are murdered by an assailant with a handgun or rifle the "Left" gets excited. If you've never noticed go back and read their post-tragedy Tweets. It is their time to talk about "gun control." Guns are a subject that VERY few of them know anything about.

The meme above exposes a common fallacy that people on the Left, and even some on the Right, love to spew. I don't know how many times I've heard that to turn an AR-15 or AK-47 rifle into a "fully automatic machine-gun" all you need is a file. I'm sorry but it doesn't work that way as you can see. One has way more parts to its trigger group.

Speaking of "triggers," imagine how a Leftist loses their minds when you explain this to them. I even saw a woman on Twitter respond to a man that corrected Hillary Clinton on how suppressors work by accusing him of "mansplaning" [sic]. They cannot accept correction or criticism.

It's clear that the Left will not only talk without all the facts, but will also lie to push their agenda, all the while pretending to be experts on every "pet policy." The more educated you are on their trigger subjects (health care, gun control etc.) the better you will be able to shut them down with facts and logic. Study up, it's a good time!

Day 27 – Creating "Black Markets"

The State and its lackeys work diligently to prove to us that they only have our "best interests" at heart. They care so much for us that they have constructed laws to protect us from ourselves. Never mind that these laws are so selective (i.e., alcohol is good, marijuana is bad) that even the most hard-hearted statist can see through their charade.

When the State decides that something people desire is "harmful" and needs to be regulated, a black market can develop to provide for the demand. Recent history has shown us that this void is filled by people that are forced to use violence to protect their businesses from not only rival competition, but the "troops" that the State puts on the streets to "war" against the "economy" they've created.

I recently heard, "if it weren't for the I.R.S they never would've stopped Al Capone." Well, if it weren't for Prohibition we never would've *heard* of him!

Prohibition not only creates an underground market, but it also leads to issues with quality control. An acquaintance told me recently that a high school friend of his got ahold of some bad "moonshine" and was in the hospital suffering delusions. That's today, when alcohol is legal. Go read some of the stories from the Twenties, they're tragic. Today we have "alternative" marijuana that is supposed to be invisible on drug tests. The horror stories from it are endless.

Prohibition by the State has proven to be more dangerous to life and liberty than any Free Market.

Day 28 – When You Have No Real Principles

We've all heard the parable about building your house on a solid foundation and not on a bed of shifting sand. My purpose in putting together these memes and commentaries is so that you can have a strong core of beliefs as you move forward. Each one of us succumbs to emotion but it's how we proceed once we get our head straight that's important.

I brought up "emotions" because I want to talk about "Liberals/Democrats/Resisters." You may have already noticed that they are principled when it comes to certain ideas but consistency and critically thinking a position through is not their strong suit. Let's look at the meme presented.

Again, this is being written shortly after the tragedy in Las Vegas, so they immediately jumped to their "core" issue of gun confiscation. Do you see how they don't think their arguments through? These are the people that have been screaming "resist" since Trump was elected. They have shown sympathy for ANTIFA who are out there getting violent and just might be planning revolution.

Yet, with all the talk of "resist," they want to take the one thing out of people's hands that would enable them to resist tyranny. This would be a perfect time for a facepalm meme.

Day 29 – Revisiting Crucial Information

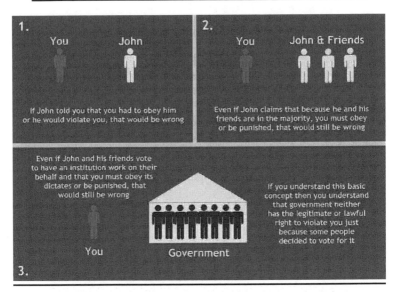

If you've been following closely you will recognize the subject of the meme above as one that I have chosen to go over more than any other. I consider it essential to liberty.

Think about the government you know (I'm going to use the U.S. as my example because it's the one I am most familiar with). If you work for an employer, a large percentage of your labor is taken every pay period. You don't even get to see it! You may say, "Oh, but I get that back at the end of the year." Do you? How do you get it back? Do you have to apply (beg)? Do you get all of it? A lot of people PAY someone else, a "tax expert," just to get THEIR money back. Why is this normal to most people?

Pretend one weekend you're lying on a lawn chair in front of your house enjoying a cold beer. A "law enforcement officer" pulls up, jumps out of the cruiser and says that you're breaking the law and you must come with him to the station. If you are 100% certain that you have broken no law can you tell him that, and demand he leave your property? Would you be confident in doing so? No? Why not? How did that man/woman get the authority to essentially kidnap you if they deem it so?

Some may say that many people need this. People are evil, and they need to be ruled. Even if I believe that, why can't I, who has self-control and leaves other people alone, opt out of this mess? Try mentioning that to a statist friend. Tell them that you want to remain in this society but be exempt from its chains. Watch their face. It's fear. In that moment they will fear you. How dare you desire freedom that they consider to be dangerous? "What are you, an anarchist?"

Day 30 – Private Sector > Public Sector

ABC News
NEWS 5 hrs · ⊘

Man in Nebraska orders pizza for his grandma in Florida to make sure she was alright after he couldn't reach her following Hurricane Matthew. "Police and fire couldn't do it, but Papa John's got there in 30 minutes and put the cellphone to her ear."

Family Sends Pizza Deliveryman to Check on Grandma After Hurricane

When your entry level, college aged, pizza guy is a more efficient rescue force than the Government

One of the main arguments you hear against a massive reduction in the State (or its complete abolishment) is that there are just some services the private sector can't provide. The sophist will jump right to "who will build the roads?" The individual who has thought more about it mentions police/fire rescue/military. Who can blame them? From a young age we are taught that the State must keep a monopoly over these things. "How would they get paid?" "If they were privatized wouldn't there be widespread corruption?" (The latter is my personal favorite)

The above meme references how on October 9, 2016, a Nebraska man who couldn't reach his grandmother in Florida used the private sector to make sure she was OK after a hurricane had hit a couple days previous. The power went out that Friday, her cell phone died and they couldn't verify her safety.

Now please UNDERSTAND this. Had the man called police or any public service, they would not have gone to check on grandma. That is not their job. Warren vs. District of Columbia decided that the police HAVE NO duty to protect you. They are not here to keep individuals safe, they are here to ENFORCE LAWS. Please research Warren vs. D.C.

Knowing that the government wouldn't help, this man called a private company to deliver a pizza so that the family would know that she was well. Upon arrival, if the driver found that grandma was in distress, then he could call an ambulance (usually another private entity) and get her the help she needed.

Incidents such as this should teach you two things:

1. The police are not there to serve you although you are paying their salary.
2. Even though Papa John's is not a rescue service, they became one because it benefitted them financially. (Maybe an idea for an after-disaster rescue service?)

Day 31 – Who Have You Ceded Control To?

So here we are at day 31. A bonus day in some months. For thirty days I have carefully laid out a pathway to guide your mind towards liberty and away from the State, culture, anything that would have you believe that you do not own yourself. I hope that I have done my job. How you use the knowledge I've shared is up to you.

Let's look at the meme. Many people within a society take as fact what they hear in the "mainstream press." So much so that if you present an alternate narrative they will not accept it unless it is echoed by their "experts" on truth. Try it. Whatever "big news story" is popular when you are reading this, mention to a friend that there may be more to the story. What reaction will you get? Almost certainly they're going to ask for a link to CNN or FOX News.

Let's use CNN as an example. Executives have admitted that they get inside information from the C.I.A. Think about that. The one thing we are sure of when it comes to the C.I.A. is that they are trained liars. We know the C.I.A. has used misinformation the world over to topple regimes and cause unrest. And this is the source people want to hold up as "truth?"

I will end this with a plea: THINK FOR YOURSELF! It takes time and effort but if you truly want to be free you will not be able to rely on other people. Not even me!

MEME GALLERY

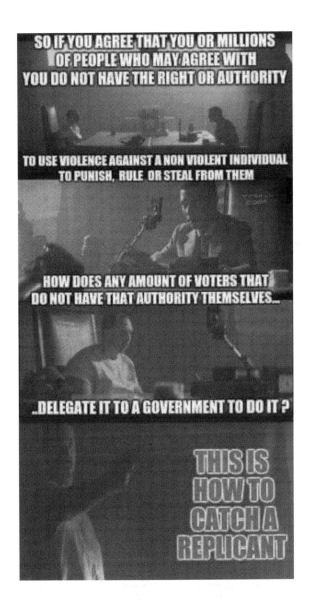

Who would win ?

The entire
collectivist ideology

One French boi

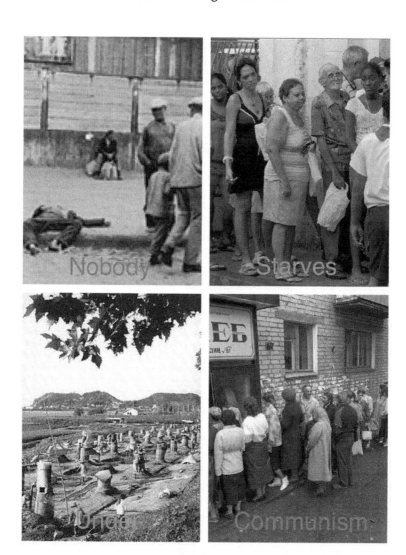

Socialism debunked in two sentences.

1 All of the socialists could meet up, gather all of their wealth together and then divide it equally between themselves.

2 This has never happened.

The endless cycle of Socialism

Insanity: doing the same thing over and over again and expecting different results.

Socialist take over

1

It wasn't real Socialism so let's do it again

3

2

Socialist system creates misery and death

THE 2ND AMENDMENT DOESN'T PROTECT YOUR RIGHT TO BEAR ARMS.

THE FUCKING GUNS DO.

THE CONSTITUTION STOPPING BIG GOVERNMENT

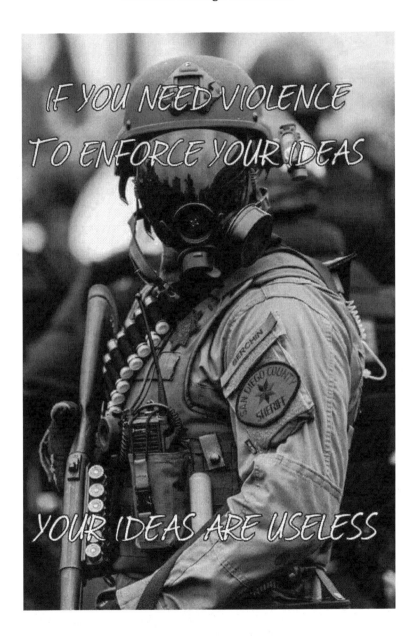

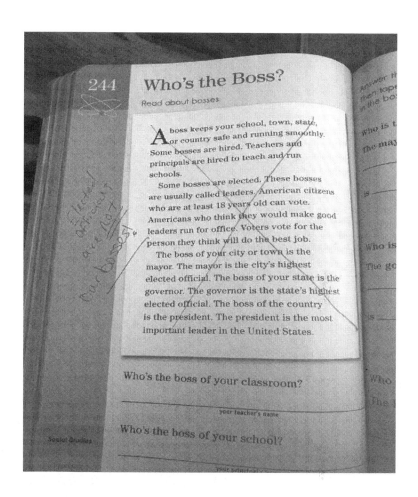

244 Who's the Boss?

Read about bosses.

A boss keeps your school, town, state, or country safe and running smoothly. Some bosses are hired. Teachers and principals are hired to teach and run schools.

Some bosses are elected. These bosses are usually called leaders. American citizens who are at least 18 years old can vote. Americans who think they would make good leaders run for office. Voters vote for the person they think will do the best job.

The boss of your city or town is the mayor. The mayor is the city's highest elected official. The boss of your state is the governor. The governor is the state's highest elected official. The boss of the country is the president. The president is the most important leader in the United States.

Who's the boss of your classroom?

_____
your teacher's name

Who's the boss of your school?

_____
your principal's name

Social Studies

Handwritten annotations: "Elected officials are not" / "Our bosses!"

Made in the USA
San Bernardino, CA
27 March 2019